Little Science

Plant Parts

By Amanda Gebhardt

2 Plant parts help plants grow.

Roots dig deep in the dirt.
Tree roots grow thick.

4 Grass roots grow wide and thin.

Plants can grow bright buds.
These buds open wide.

This bee sits and sips.
It can buzz from bud to bud.
It takes pollen for a ride.

What can pollen do? It can help the plant grow fruit.

Buds will drop. Fruit will grow.

Fruit has seeds inside.

Seeds will drop. They will grow new roots.

They will grow new stems.

They will grow new plants
with big bright buds.

And it all starts again.

Word List

science words

buds	Roots
grow	roots
fruit	seeds
Plant	Seeds
plants	stems
Plants	Tree

sight words

a	inside
again	open
all	parts
dirt	pollen
do	starts
for	the
from	to
	What

Vowel Teams

/ā/ey	/ē/ee	/ī/igh	/ō/ow	/oo/ew, oo, ui
They	bee	bright	grow	fruit
	deep			Fruit
	seeds			new
	Seeds			Roots
	Tree			roots

Try It!
How many plant parts can you find outside?
Draw pictures of what you find.

14

Plant parts help plants grow.

Roots dig deep in the dirt. Tree roots grow thick.

Grass roots grow wide and thin.

Plants can grow bright buds. These buds open wide.

This bee sits and sips. It can buzz from bud to bud.
It takes pollen for a ride.

What can pollen do? It can help the plant grow fruit.

Buds will drop. Fruit will grow.

Fruit has seeds inside.

Seeds will drop. They will grow new roots.

They will grow new stems.

They will grow new plants with big bright buds.

And it all starts again.

CHERRY BLOSSOM PRESS

Published in the United States of America by Cherry Lake Publishing Group
Ann Arbor, Michigan
www.cherrylakepublishing.com

Photo Credits: © Seesea/Dreamstime.com, cover, title page; © schame/Shutterstock, 2; © Aekawut Rattawan/Shutterstock, 3; © ER_09/Shutterstock, 4; © Elena Gavrilova/Dreamstime.com, 5; © Rehuretskyi Serhii/Shutterstock, 6; © Ivanka Kunianska/Shutterstock, 7; © Sikth/Dreamstime.com, 8; © Sergey Denisov/Dreamstime.com, 9, back cover; © Janis Smits/Shutterstock, 10; j.chizhe/Shutterstock, 11; © Sokolan495/Dreamstime.com, 12; © Tanaonte/Dreamstime.com, 13

Cherry Blossom Press is an imprint of Cherry Lake Publishing Group.

Library of Congress Cataloging-in-Publication Data

Names: Gebhardt, Amanda, author.
Title: Plant parts / written by: Amanda Gebhardt.
Description: Ann Arbor, Michigan : Cherry Blossom Press, [2024] | Series:
   Little science stories | Audience: Grades K-1 | Summary: "Learn about
   plant parts in this decodable science book for beginning readers. A
   combination of domain-specific sight words and sequenced phonics skills
   builds confidence in content area reading. Bold, colorful photographs
   align directly with the text to help readers strengthen comprehension"—
   Provided by publisher.
Identifiers: LCCN 2023035053 | ISBN 9781668937662 (paperback) | ISBN
   9781668940044 (ebook) | ISBN 9781668941393 (pdf)
Subjects: LCSH: Plant anatomy—Juvenile literature.
Classification: LCC QK641 .G34 2024 | DDC 571.3/2—dc23/eng/20230818
LC record available at https://lccn.loc.gov/2023035053

Printed in the United States of America

Amanda Gebhardt is a curriculum writer and editor and a life-long learner. She lives in Ann Arbor, Michigan, with her husband, two kids, and one playful pup named Cookie.